ESTONIA TRAVEL GUIDE 2023

Embarking on an Unforgettable Journey to Estonia's Vibrant Culture, Breathtaking Scenery, and Cutting-Edge Technology: A Travel Guide for 2023

HARRY WHITE

All right reserved.

No part of this publication may be reduced, distributed, or transmitted in any form or by any means, including photocopying, recording, or any other electronic or mechanical methods, without the prior written permission of the publisher, except in the case of brief quotations embodied in critical reviews and certain other non-commercial uses permitted by copyright law.

Copyright @ Harry White, 2023

Table Of Content

Introduction
Welcome To Estonia
Brief History Of Estonia
Location Of Estonia On The Map
Reasons To Visit Estonia
Things to Know Before Visiting Estonia
Top-Rated Attraction In Estonia (Landmark)
Cities And Vacation In Estonia
The Food And Dishes In Estonia
Estonia Tourist Visa Required Documents
Best Time To Visit Estonia
The Ideal 3-Day Trip Itinerary To Estonia
Estonia Travel Cost
Cultural Do's & Don'ts
Culture and social etiquette in Estonia
Accommodations in Estonia
Transportation in Estonia
Safety and Security
Best Restaurants In Estonia
Nightlife And Clubs in Estonia
Conclusion

Introduction

I had always been curious about the small country of Estonia in Northern Europe. So, when the opportunity to travel there presented itself, I jumped at the chance.

As I stepped off the plane in Tallinn, the capital city, I was immediately struck by the picturesque architecture and the charm of the cobblestone streets.

I began my adventure by exploring the city's historic Old Town, which is a UNESCO World Heritage Site.

I wandered through the winding alleyways, admiring the colorful buildings and Gothic spires that towered above. I stopped for a traditional Estonian lunch at a cozy café and indulged in Kama, a local dish made from roasted barley, rye, and peas.

After lunch, I visited the Kumu Art Museum, which showcases Estonian art from the 18th century to the present. I was particularly fascinated by the contemporary art exhibitions, which featured works by local artists.

I also visited the Museum of Occupations, which tells the story of Estonia's occupation by the Soviet Union and Nazi Germany, giving me a deeper understanding of the country's complex history.

My next stop was the Lahemaa National Park, where I spent the day hiking through the pristine forests and along the rugged coastline.

I marveled at the stunning landscapes and the abundance of wildlife, from moose and lynx to seals and seabirds. I even had the chance to spot some of the rare plant species that grow only in Estonia.

The highlight of my trip, however, was my visit to Saaremaa Island. The island's peaceful and idyllic countryside was a welcome contrast to the hustle and bustle of the city.

I rented a bicycle and rode through the picturesque landscapes, stopping to admire the windmills and quaint fishing villages.

I even got to try my hand at traditional Estonian handicrafts, such as weaving and pottery, at a local workshop.

As my trip came to an end, I reflected on my unforgettable experience in Estonia. I discovered a new and unique travel destination that exceeded all my expectations.

I had been captivated by the country's natural beauty, impressed by its rich cultural heritage, and charmed by its warm and friendly people. I knew that I would never forget my time in Estonia and that I would always look back on it with fondness and a desire to return.

Estonia City

Welcome To Estonia

Estonia, a hidden gem in Northern Europe, offers travelers a unique blend of history, culture, and natural beauty.

With its rich heritage, vibrant cities, and picturesque countryside, Estonia is a destination that caters to a variety of interests and preferences. As you plan your travels for 2023, consider adding Estonia to your list of must-visit destinations.

The capital city of Tallinn is the most popular tourist destination in Estonia and for good reason.

This charming medieval city is a UNESCO World Heritage Site and is renowned for its well-preserved Old Town, cobbled streets, and historic landmarks.

Here you can wander through the winding alleyways, visit the many museums and art galleries, and indulge in the local cuisine and nightlife.

Beyond Tallinn, Estonia has much more to offer. The country's natural beauty is best explored through its national parks, such as Lahemaa and Soomaa, which feature rugged coastlines, pristine forests, and serene lakes.

Estonia's numerous islands, such as Saaremaa and Hiiumaa, are also popular destinations for their unique landscapes, wildlife, and cultural heritage.

Estonia's rich cultural history is reflected in its festivals, museums, and architecture.

The Song Festival, held every five years, is a celebration of Estonia's choral tradition and brings together thousands of singers and musicians from all over the country.

The Museum of Occupations in Tallinn tells the story of Estonia's occupation by the Soviet Union and Nazi Germany, while the Kumu Art Museum showcases Estonian art from the 18th century to the present.

Whether you're interested in history, culture, or nature, Estonia has something to offer. With its diverse range of attractions, Estonia is an ideal destination for travelers seeking an immersive and authentic experience.

So, if you're looking to discover a new and unique travel destination in 2023, Estonia should be on your list.

Brief History Of Estonia

Estonia's history stretches back over 10,000 years to the arrival of the first hunter-gatherers in the region.

Throughout its history, Estonia has been shaped by its strategic location between East and West, and by the successive waves of conquerors and traders who passed through the region.

In the Middle Ages, Estonia was ruled by a series of foreign powers, including the Danes, Germans, and Swedes.

The country's rich cultural heritage is reflected in its many historic landmarks, such as the ancient hill fortresses of Toompea and Narva, and the well-preserved medieval Old Town of Tallinn.

In the 20th century, Estonia experienced a tumultuous period of occupation and oppression, first under Soviet rule and then under Nazi occupation during World War II.

After the war, Estonia was once again occupied by the Soviet Union and remained under Soviet control until it regained independence in 1991.

Since then, Estonia has undergone a remarkable transformation, becoming one of the most prosperous and technologically advanced countries in Europe.

Estonia joined the European Union in 2004 and has since become a leading player in the fields of e-government and digital innovation.

Today, Estonia is a vibrant and dynamic country that continues to draw visitors from all over the world with its unique blend of history, culture, and natural beauty.

Whether you're interested in exploring its medieval cities, hiking through its national parks, or experiencing its thriving arts and culture scene, Estonia has something to offer everyone.

Interesting Fun Fact

The forest cover on Estonian territory exceeds 50%.

Yes, this indicates that there aren't many people in the area. The astonishing biodiversity is another result of this. More than 70 distinct species may live in a square meter of forested meadows. Watch your step, then!

There is a prize-winning oak tree in Saaremaa.

Saaremaa, an oak tree in Orissaare's midst of a football field, garnered over 60,000 votes and was named the 2015 European Tree of the Year. That is a staggering 32% of all votes cast. Everyone in Estonia was happy.

In Estonia, there are 7,000 rivers, 1,000 lakes, and 1,500 islands.

If you're looking for something completely different, Estonia boasts the most meteorite craters per square kilometer in the whole globe. The last massive meteorite to strike a region with a human population left behind the Kaali crater in Saaremaa. Over 4,000 years ago, it descended to Earth with the force of a nuclear bomb.

With a height of 318 meters, Suur Munamägi (Big Egg Hill) is the highest point in the Baltic area.

Suur Munamägi was allegedly created by the giant Kalevipoeg as a cushion to lay his head on, according to a legend found in the Estonian national epic Kalevipoeg.

Even if this myth lacks supporting documentation, the hill is still around six meters higher than Latvia's highest point, which gives its northern neighbors great pride.

singing individuals: With approximately 133,000 songs, Estonia has the world's biggest collection of national folk music.

The Tallinn Song Festival, which takes place every five years, is renowned for having the most simultaneous choral singers on stage.

Over 200 000 people attend the event, 34,000 individuals perform together, and up to 18,000 people may be on stage at once.

This is almost one-sixth of the whole population!Spa junkies should know that Kuressaare, Estonia, is the world's spa capital, with over 1,200 spa beds for every 15,000 residents.

Since the time of the tsars, Estonia has been "the place" for spa treatments because of its abundance of mud baths, saunas, and sea air.

The settlements of Haapsalu and Narva-Jesuu were well-known in the 19th century due to its curative mud, in addition to their pine woods and virgin beaches.

You may participate in the heated sauna competition.

Sauna use is ingrained in Estonian culture. a manner of living naturally. A sauna is a common home feature that is utilized at least once each week.

You may even set up a sauna tent or take a sauna bus if you're on the road. Particularly well-liked is the yearly Otepää sauna race, which combines orienteering with saunas in the midst of winter.

Winners and record breakers

The 2001 Eurovision Song Contest was won by Estonia.
Even the Estonians were taken aback by the victory.

The world's largest concentration of international supermodels per person is found in Estonia.
It's difficult to choose just a few females from among Estonia's top-known models.

Let's simply say that Carmen Kass and Karmen Pedaru are from these regions of the globe, among others.

An Estonian is the world champion wife-carrier (yes, there is such a thing!).

Even though Estonia is a very egalitarian nation, we nonetheless develop skilled wife carriers. Additionally, you should look into kicking if strange sports are your thing.

Kicking involves athletes trying to complete a full 360-degree turn around the top bar of the swing while mounted on enormous swings.

The one who can accomplish it on the swing with the longest swing arms is the winner.
In 2011, Tallinn served as the European Capital of Culture.
Every year, the EU names a city as the European Capital of Culture.

This enables the chosen towns to develop their cultures and introduce them to the outside world. Together with Turku, Finland, Tallinn co-hosted approximately 250 cultural events throughout the year, including the performing arts, film, literature, sports, and other disciplines.

Moving forward with e-Estonia
Estonia accepted internet voting in 2005, when other nations were still debating it.

In this country, firms may be formed in only a few minutes and 95% of tax returns are submitted online.

With the advent of mobile IDs, anybody residing outside of Estonia may now use their ID card or mobile ID to sign legally binding papers.

And it's true that you can obtain 4G coverage even deep in the woods.
In Europe, Estonia has the most new businesses per person.

Estonia has the 132nd-smallest land area in the world. Yet it generates more start-ups per capita than any other nation in Europe, according to the Wall Street Journal. We are the source of

While rivers, lakes, and the ocean are teeming with mouthwatering fish like salmon and sea trout, forests are rife with tasty edibles like blueberries, cloudberries, and mushrooms. You may enjoy farm-to-table dining in Estonia!

Internet accessibility

With free wifi connections available everywhere, Estonia ensures that all tourists may tweet and snap about how amazing Estonia is in a world where everyone must be connected at all times by phone, laptop, or tablet.

It's a paradise for travel bloggers and digital nomads! Great businesses like Skype and Hotmail were founded in Estonia.

It is not surprising that this little nation in the Baltics is the world's most technologically proficient digital civilization. Even complicated tasks like voting and healthcare are completed quickly.

Accessible, wild, and unaltered nature

One would assume that a nation this technologically and economically developed wouldn't be very green or endowed with a wealth of natural resources, yet Estonia is really one of the greenest nations in the world.

With woods covering roughly half of the land, Estonia's unspoiled natural splendor is accessible to nature enthusiasts everywhere.

No Mass Tourism

If you've ever visited well-known European cities like Rome, Venice, Amsterdam, or Vienna during the summer, you are aware of how packed and crowded they can get.

However, if you visit Estonia, you won't have to worry about that since even the "touristy" city of Tallinn is far less congested than many other European cities. Once you leave the city center, you can even be the only visitor there.

It's simple to navigate

Because Estonia is so tiny, it's the perfect site for tourists to go even farther off the beaten track and see all Estonia has to offer.

With easy access to public transportation, villages and cities including Tartu, Värska, Viljandi, and Haapsalu are fantastic day excursions from the capital.

Europe's Best Value for Your Money

In all of Europe, Estonia provides the finest value for your money.

For the same price as some typical cafés in Scandinavia, you can eat at White Guide Nordic-class mall restaurants in Egypt. I don't know what will persuade you to go to Estonia if it doesn't.

Historical Nation

Due to its past as a part of the Soviet Union and the Swedish, Russian, and German occupations, Estonia has a unique history, a thriving culture, and stunning architecture.

Wherever you travel in Estonia, you will still be able to see traces of historical monuments, customs, and traditions, notably in the capital city of Tallinn. One of Northern Europe's best-preserved medieval cities is Tallinn. Estonia is a must-see if you like history.

Everyone Can Find Something in Estonia

A wide variety of attractions may be found in Estonia. Whatever your hobbies, travel preferences, or financial limitations, there is something for you to adore and enjoy in Estonia.

One day you may be trekking through the forest eating wild berries, the next you could be visiting a castle or relaxing on the beach.

It would be a pity to lose out on everything that this little Baltic nation has to offer, so maybe we have persuaded you to make Estonia your next holiday destination.

Things to Know Before Visiting Estonia

Beautiful Architecture

The amazing diversity of architecture I was able to see while touring Estonia's cities and villages was perhaps one of the things I most loved.

It seemed as if there were structures from almost every era of the nation's history, which is no minor accomplishment for a nation that has seen several invasions and occupations throughout the years.

Tallinn Old Town is the place to go if you're interested in medieval architecture. Then there are Tartu's exquisite Neoclassical structures, like the above-pictured pink and scarlet Town Hall.

In the districts of Tallinn and Tartu, as well as in beautiful wood panel homes by the sea in areas like Pärnu, you may see 19th-century working-class residences. However, there are

Top-Rated Attraction In Estonia (Landmark)

The country of Estonia should be on your short list of travel destinations if you're searching for a change of pace from the conventional European trip.

This former Soviet state, one of the least populous in Europe, is filled to the brim with intact medieval towns, magical woods, hazy bogs, and old customs. It's like a scene from a fairy tale come to reality.

Your experiences will probably begin in Tallinn, the capital of Estonia, where there are a lot of things to do.

You may stroll around the ancient city walls, consume endless quantities of black bread from Estonia, explore the Russian Orthodox Cathedral, and see the whole city from the Tallinn TV Tower.

After that, go out and discover more of what this little yet powerful nation has to offer. Get treated in the opulent baths in Pärnu, the summer capital of Estonia.

Take out your binoculars in Matsalu National Park, one of the greatest bird-watching locations on earth. Ride a bicycle along the lovely Narva River Promenade. And after you've gotten your fill of Estonia's mainland, travel to one of the country's more than 2,000 islands.

In this beautiful location, boredom is not an option. Our list of the best things to do in Estonia will help you organize your sightseeing.

Pärnu

Pärnu, which is only a two-hour drive from Tallinn, entices visitors with its stunning coastline and cozy atmosphere.

Any of the town's many spas will pamper you from head to toe, but the Hedon SPA & Hotel offers a particularly remarkable experience.

The spa is close to 200 years old and provides therapeutic mud wraps that clear pores and leave skin velvety smooth. It is the oldest of its type in Estonia. Relax in the saunas, saltwater pool, and summer patio after your treatment.

Don't pass up the chance to explore the 1265-year-old medieval town, which has been magnificently conserved. You may arrange to meet a qualified tour guide who will show you about Pärnu via the tourist information office.

Historic maps, hidden passageways, a centuries-old home that once belonged to the town's blacksmith, a statue of Estonian architect Olev Siinmaa, and memorials to Johann Voldemar Jannsen—the "father of Estonian journalism" and the creator of one of the nation's oldest still-published newspapers—will all be found here.

For those who wish to explore Kihnu Island, Pärnu makes a fantastic base. The island, which is home to a small community of 700 people, most of whom are women, is renowned for its long-standing musical and singing traditions that go back a thousand years.

Watch out for the elderly ladies riding antique motorbikes around the island while dressed traditionally; it's a cute sight.

The Old Town of Tallin

You should spend as much time as your itinerary will allow seeing Tallinn's Old Town, regardless of whether your trip to Estonia is a lengthy holiday or simply a one-day stop on a Baltic cruise.

Rich merchants from Germany and Denmark lived there in the 13th century, and it is one of the best-preserved Hanseatic town centers in the whole globe.

Postal code: Vesilennuki tänav 6, Phja-Tallinna linnaosa, Tallinn

National Museum of Estonia

The Estonian National Museum is highly known for both its striking architecture and its engaging permanent displays on Estonian history and culture.

The structure, a work of conceptual art that debuted in 2016 on a former Soviet military installation, was modeled as an airstrip that was flying off into space.

It is extremely spectacular at night because of the lights.

Give yourself at least two hours to examine the museum's treasures. The primary permanent exhibit, "Encounters," offers visitors a glimpse into everyday Estonian life and culture from the Ice Age to the present.

The Finno-Ugric peoples are the subject of "Echo of the Urals," the museum's second ongoing display.

It features an impressive array of everyday items like kitchenware and apparel from other cultures. The museum's high-tech displays enhance the participatory nature of the experience.

Address: Tartu, Estonia, Muuseumi tee 2

National Park of Matsalu

Visitors who are considering visiting Estonia should remember to bring their binoculars. One of Europe's top bird-watching locations is said to be the nation's Matsalu National Park.

A protected natural habitat for breeding, molting, and migratory birds, including the spectacular white-tailed eagle, covers its 48,610 hectares. More than 22 protected plant species may be found in the park, along with 10 animals that are being safeguarded.

In Haeska, Keemu, Kloostri, and other sections of the park, there are a number of bird-watching towers from which visitors may obtain a panoramic view of this stunning region.

A few hiking routes that pass through marshes, coastal pastures, and meadows are also available for your enjoyment.

You may experience the region's most breathtaking time of day—sunrise—by staying at one of the park's guesthouses.

Its Park

Oru Park near the town of Toila in northern Estonia is a tranquil retreat tucked away in the lovely Pühajgi River valley.

The wealthy Russian guy who developed the park in the 19th century had a royal sense of style. Consider hypnotic-shaped topiary gardens, charming fountains, observation stations on balconies, and plenty of flowers.

If you're going to Oru Park in the summer, bring a swimsuit. There is a trail that leads to a lovely pebble beach, which is ideal for sunbathing and swimming.

Continue to relax after your stay at the renowned Toila Baths. Along with Jacuzzi pools, the day spa offers a range of saunas, including infrared, aromatherapy, and salty air. The whole room has an antique Rome-like air about it.

The following address: Oru tänav-21, Toila alevik, Toila valid, Ida-Viru maakond

Castle Episcopal in Kuressaare

The moat-ringed Kuressaare Episcopal Castle has stood tall since the 1380s and is one of the best-preserved fortifications in the Baltic area.

You may spend the whole day exploring the castle's many distinctive areas, such as the convent building, narrow stairs, central courtyard, cloister, refectory, and the bishop's residence, which is home to 11 Baroque wood sculptures.

You can also spend time taking in the Gothic ambiance of the Gothic-style architecture. Enjoy a delicious meal while admiring the scenery at the Tower Cafe.

Through exhibits of unique objects (including more than 2,000 ancient coins dating back to the 1620s), the on-site history museum provides insight into life over the many decades that this castle was in use.

During the busy summer months, visitors may also see and take part in traditional activities including archery, pottery making, musical performances, and firing Estonia's oldest operational cannon.

Make reservations for the castle's Bishop's Dinner if you're visiting in a group. A display of traditional table etiquette from centuries ago is included in the two-hour gourmet event, which also includes foods prepared using old recipes and beverages served in goblets.

Saaremaa valid, Saare maakond, Lossihoov 1, Kuressaare linn

River Promenade at Narva

The fantastic gazing options along the Narva River Promenade are unmatched by many other locations in Estonia.

The Narva River, which forms a natural border between Russia and the European Union, has a riverside boardwalk that is over a kilometer long.

There is always something intriguing and lovely to view along the peaceful promenade. You can see the bastion walls and the Hermann Castle, a stone building from the fourteenth century, to the west. North of the promenade, the Narva harbor dominates the landscape.

Visitors may also go to the Joaorg recreation area in the south, which contains a beach house. You may hire bikes, sun loungers, volleyball sets, and badminton courts at this location.

The promenade is a great place to spend a day riding or strolling while taking in the fly fishermen and the sunset.

Location: Je tänav, Narva

Mount Toompea

You should ascend Toompea Hill while you wander around Tallinn's Old Town. Folklore in Estonia holds that the hill guards the resting place of a legendary monarch called Kalev, whose 12 sons are said to be the cause of mysterious occurrences in the natural world.

The town is connected to the hill's summit by a 157-step stairway, and many observation platforms there provide breathtaking views of the whole city.

The Toompea Castle, a beautiful pink structure that houses the Estonian parliament's offices, is located nearby. On weekdays, you may take a tour of the castle or watch parliament proceedings from the public gallery (prior reservations are necessary).

Make sure to gaze at the flag flying from the Tall Hermann tower of the castle, which is regarded as a significant symbol of Estonian freedom.

Science Center AHHAA

Not your usual scientific museum, the AHHAA scientific Center in Tartu is unique.

The 3,000 square meter area provides hands-on exhibitions visitors can engage with, making science exciting and magical, rather than placing displays behind glass.

In the Hall of Technology, visitors may ride a bike over a high rope, navigate a maze of mirrors, and take pictures while exploding balloons.

The many wildlife from throughout the globe are highlighted at the Hall of Nature. A colony of 20,000 wood ants, schools of tropical fish in a 6,000-liter tank, and other entertaining exhibits may be found in that permanent exhibit.

Visitors are also welcome to observe cute chicks emerge from their eggs at the museum.

Plan your visit to coincide with one of the breathtaking planetarium shows, which transport guests to a distant galaxy.

Sadama tänav 1 in Tartu Linn, Estonia

Cities And Vacation In Estonia

Top tourist destinations in Estonia include a wide range of activities, places to visit, and other attractions, including:
- Estonian castles
- residences in manors
- historical sites
- Lovely natural beaches
- Seasonal celebrations
- architecture and monuments from the Soviet period

Additionally, you may discover quaint cafés and eateries, museums that can help you learn about the local history, and stores that offer handcrafted trinkets and presents.

Rakvere

Rakvere's magnificent castle remains, which holds festivals, draw plenty of tourists. Another

Estonian city that is committed to sustainability and green living is Rakvere, where trash reduction and energy efficiency are advantages for both locals and visitors.

The canvas, or auroch, sculpture, which honors the 700th anniversary of the establishment of this Estonian city, can be located next to the castle.

The 17th century saw the construction of the medieval church with the lofty spire.

Rakvere is close to Lahemaa National Park, which offers many chances for hikers, bird watchers, and other nature lovers.

Rakvere

Tallinn

The most northern of the three capitals of the Baltic states is Tallinn, the capital of Estonia.

Tallinn is a wonderful blend of the ancient and the modern. Visitors are won over by the Old Town Tallinn's ancient alleys and breathtaking scenery.

In the meanwhile, its variety of communities, each with a distinct attitude, enables visitors to go farther away.

For instance, the artsy and bohemian Telliskivi neighborhood is covered with street art. The Rotermann area provides locations for companies, cafés, restaurants, and stores while elegantly integrating modern construction within a historic district.

Tallinn, the nation's capital, doubles as its center of culture. Concerts, festivals, and exhibits may be found here any day or night. Visit Estonia at Easter or take in the Christmas market in Tallinn.

Without a question, one of the best things to do in Estonia is to visit Tallinn.

Tallinn

Viljandi

The greatest city in Estonia for festivals is Viljandi, which is situated in the country's south. One of its most popular events is the Viljandi Folk Music Festival.

The Bonifatius Guild shop sells a selection of handcrafted goods manufactured by artisans, including works of Baltic folk art.

Visitors to this town also come for its natural landscape, the centerpiece of which is a lake surrounded by trees. They also come for the town's wooden architecture.

Viljandi

Tartu

Estonia's university town is Tartu. It's also the second-largest city in Estonia, yet it still has a warm, homely vibe.

Tartu is worth visiting for its riverfront promenade, wooden buildings, and Estonian National Museum.

It's simple to go to Tartu by rail from Tallinn for a delightful day excursion. Everything in Tartu makes you feel at home, from the main plaza to the cathedral ruins to the park with its old trees.

Tartu

Kuressaare

Saaremaa Island contains Kuressaare. Probably its most well-known landmark is its former medieval fortification, which is now a museum. Its main plaza is attractive and has antique buildings.

Churches, manor buildings, and windmills may all be found on Estonia's largest island, which can easily be explored from Kuressaare.

Haapsalu

Another Estonian city with a reputation for spas is Haapsalu. Haapsalu is a warm and inviting seaside town that is as popular a vacation spot now as it was in the past.

The Shawl Museum, which is devoted to the beautiful lace shawls manufactured in the area for decades, is one of several museums that let tourists learn more about the city and its residents, both past and present.

A medieval castle is also located at Haapsalu.

Haapsalu

Narva

One of Estonia's most fascinating cities is Narva. It is situated in Estonia's northeast, not far from the Russian border. This indicates that there are many Russian speakers there.

Along with being located in Narva, Narva Castle is an Estonian fortress that competes with Russia's Ivangorod Fortress across the Narva River. Here, it seems that competition from the Middle Ages still exists now.

Parnu

The fourth-largest city in the nation and one of the most popular tourist destinations in Estonia is Parnu. As a seaside community, Parnu will win your heart if you like spending time on the beach, even in the cool Baltic Sea.

The statue of Johann Voldemar Jannsen, a significant figure in the Estonian Independence struggle, is among its well-known attractions.

It is well renowned for its spas and boasts a beautiful historic town that is ideal for exploring in addition to its seaside promenade.

Parnu

The Food And Dishes In Estonia

Vürtsikilu Suupiste: Spicy Sprats Snack

Sprats are a tasty, little oily fish that resembles sardines. They are used in various meals in Estonia and are quite popular there.

The majority of your neighborhood supermarkets and grocery shops carry sprats. They are available pre-smoked, in cans, or pickled in a hot brine. Each one contributes distinct, new tastes to the dish.

Popular in Estonia is a meal called Vürtsikilu Suupiste. It's a filling sandwich that's ideal as a snack or an appetizer.

Spread a thick layer of cream cheese and smashed garlic on a piece of rye bread.

A filet of pickled sprat is put on top of the cheese and garlic base. Slices of green onion, dill, and cooked egg white are the sandwich's final toppings.

Although this snack is highly spicy, the brine's spiciness gives it a richer taste.

Strong alcoholic beverages, usually vodka of an Estonian provenance, are frequently consumed with Vürtsikilu Suupiste. Many people like this hearty Estonian cuisine.

Spicy Sprats Snack

Salad with Mixed Beets - Rosolje

Under the USSR administration, rosolje, or mixed beet salad, rose to prominence in Estonian cuisine.

Many Estonian festivities feature it. It is a straightforward meal made using the two Estonian staples, herring and beets.

Rosolje is often confused with its Russian relative, the "dressed herring," also known as "елдка од уо."

However, resolve is a far more straightforward salad than dressed herring, which is a stacked salad made up of layers of shredded vegetables and chopped pickled herring.

In the same basin, the ingredients are well combined. It has a wide variety of tastes and textures as a result.

Making rosolje is easy. Cubed pickled herring, cucumbers, boiled potatoes, beets, carrots, and eggs are all combined with mayonnaise before serving.

It is quite easy to prepare and flavorful. It's lovely to look at the colors as well.

And because of how easy it is to make and how inexpensive the ingredients are, it is quite well-liked across Estonia.

You won't be let down if you stop by a café in Estonia and get a dish of determination.

Sült's Meat Jelly

Another inventive Estonian cuisine is sült. It is made by boiling down animal bones, letting the liquid cool, and then congealing the broth with natural gelatin.

The broth is supplemented with aromatics, slices of vegetables, and pieces of meat. After cooling, a jelly slowly begins to take shape.

Aspic, also known as meat jelly, is a dish that originated in the Slavic area but is now popular around the world. It goes by the name "олоде" in Russia.

It is often offered around Christmas or Easter in Estonia. With some excellent horseradish and sour cream, sült is delicious.

Sült's Meat Jelly

Hernesupp Suitsukoodiga's Pea Soup with Smoked Pork Hock

Traditional Estonian soup known as Hernesupp Suitsukoodiga is often made on New Year's Eve.

Onions, garlic, and smoked pig bones are cooked to make the broth foundation.

Then, dried peas are added and simmered in the broth until tender. In certain versions, the soup is pureed to give it a creamier texture, and carrots may also be included.

Although Hernesupp Suitsukoodiga is an acquired taste, older Estonian generations love it very much. They are transported back in time by the taste of smoked pork and the aromas.

Eesti Kartulisalat, or potato salad from Estonia

In much of Europe, potato salad is a common dish, and each country has its own variation on it.

In Estonia, cooked potatoes and carrots are first chopped into bite-sized pieces before being added to potato salad.

The salad is then completed by the addition of a grated boiled egg, cucumber cubes, and smoked sausage.

The components are combined with a sour cream and mayonnaise sauce, and canned peas are often used as well.

Apple slices are the last component, adding a touch of sweetness. Slices of cucumber and apple work together to provide some sweetness to the savory foundation.

Estonians from all areas of life like this salad. One of Estonia's most beloved foods, it is a real national staple.

Seapraad ja Hautatud Hapukapsad (pork roast with sauerkraut)

Pork dish seapraad ja hautatud hapukapsad is healthful and filling. It's a great illustration of how Central European food influenced Estonian cooking.

It is called "eberka Wieprzowe" in Poland, where pork roast with sauerkraut first appeared.

In Estonia, during the long, chilly winters, this meal is highly well-liked. This hearty and tasty meat and vegetable mixture is ideal for feeding big groups of people as well as families.

The pork is first cooked separately in the oven until it is done but still soft and has a lot of juices.

Juices and trimmings are drained after the pig has been roasted. The sauerkraut and carrots are then put in a big saucepan with these.

The sauerkraut is carefully cooked in this mixture until it is tender. It's now prepared to be served and eaten.

It is a highly full and hearty Estonian dish. When you visit Estonia, I urge you to give it a try.

Vastlakukkel - Semla

A typical sweet roll from the Nordic areas is called a semla. Laskiaispulla and fastelavnsboller are the names for it in Finland and Denmark, respectively.

Estonian vastlakukkel is typically prepared around Shrove Tuesday and sold from the end of February to the first week of March.

In Estonia, semla is prepared with a cardamom-spiced wheat bun. The top of the bun is first cut off.

The bun has a hollow inside. Then, whipped cream that has been sweetened is added, and the cut-off top is dusted with sugar.

The whipped cream is placed on top of the sliced bun roof. It is quite flavorful and has a delicate appearance.

Similar to how you would add cream and jam to a British scone, some Estonians like adding cranberry jam to the filling.

Dessert Vastlakukkel is a delicious treat. It's a dish that Estonians eagerly anticipate eating once springtime comes and the chilly winter has ended.

Semla

Estonia Tourist Visa Required Documents

There are a number of necessary papers that you must present while applying for an Estonian visa. Depending on the kind of Estonian visa you apply for, there may be restrictions. To get a visa, you must always make sure you submit all the necessary paperwork.

When requesting an Estonian visa, you must provide the following documentation:

- Authentic passport.
- a request form.
- a receipt for the visa cost.
- two images sized for passports.
- insurance for travelers with a Schengen visa.
- resume letter.
- Flight schedule.
- evidence of accommodations.
- legal standing.
- Financial statement.

- Request letter.
- depending on your work status, documents.
- Genuine Passport

The Estonian embassy requires the following for your passport to be deemed completely valid:

- Three months or more should have passed before the return date.
- with a minimum of two empty pages.
- in excellent shape.
- a copy of any prior visas.

Visa Application Form for Estonia

The Application form has to be completed in its entirety before being signed. Make sure the application form is filled out completely and accurately.

Don't forget to fill in all the blanks. Any missing information might result in the denial of your visa.

Proof of Payment of Visa Fees

The payment of the application fee comes after completing the application form. When presenting the required paperwork, you may pay the visa application fee for Estonia at the embassy or consulate.

Depending on the kind of visa you apply for, your age, the nation you reside in, etc The visa fee payment may fluctuate.

Two images in passport form

You must submit two similar pictures that comply with the requirements for a Schengen visa. The images must be passport-sized, in color, with a light backdrop, etc., and must have been taken within the last six months.

Insurance for travelers with a Schengen visa

You must have current travel health insurance in order to apply for an Estonian visa. The following conditions must be met by your health insurance:

Valid across the whole Schengen Zone.

$30,001 in insurance.

Valid during the whole of your stay.

Case Study

The cover letter you submit with your visa application helps the Estonian embassy or consulate get to know you and learn more about why you're visiting. The cover letter must include details on inquiries like:

Why do you intend to go to Estonia?

Your arrival and departure times.

Do you intend to go to any other Schengen nations?

Your job situation?

Flight Schedule

A ticket for a flight counts as one of the needed papers. The flight ticket is documentation that attests to your departure and arrival times, as well as your return. However, you can get a flight itinerary if you don't want to purchase a ticket.

An itinerary for a flight contains the following information about you:

- Date and time of the flight.
- named aircraft.
- Date and time of arrival and departure.
- your flight's ticket cost.
- IATA airport codes.

Evidence of Housing in Estonia

A document known as the accommodation proof demonstrates that you have a place to stay when visiting Estonia. This record may be:

- Contract for renting.
- booking a hotel.
- a letter of invitation from a friend, relative, etc.
- confirmation letter from a vacation trip or organized tour company.

Civil Status Records

The following papers are required for a visa application: Marriage certificate (if you are married).

- birth certificate for your kid, if you have one.
- If you and your spouse cohabitate (shared bank account, renting agreement).

Banking Records

Additionally, you need to send your six-month worth of bank statements. This paper aims to demonstrate your ability to support yourself while remaining in Estonia and your financial stability.

If you get an invitation letter from a friend or relative who lives in Estonia and wishes to pay for your vacation, this document does not apply. You will then need an invitation letter.

Letter of Invitation from a Host in Estonia

An invitation letter is a letter that asks you to visit or stay with a friend or family member who is currently living in Estonia. This letter demonstrates that you have a place to reside as well as your legal right to do so in Estonia, which is likely the most crucial point.

- The letter must include the following, depending on the reason for your visit:

- When the letter was written, on what day.
- name of the embassy.
- Name, last name, and passport number of the applicant.
- Information about the host's residency in Estonia, including name, surname, address, and email.
- the reason for the journey.
- a connection between the two parties.
- dates of the applicant's flights and return date.

Depending on Your Employment Status.

Documents you need to provide the following information while requesting an Estonian visa, depending on your job situation:

If you have a job:

- Work agreement.
- Bank records.
- evidence that you pay taxes.

- Your employer's letter of approval demonstrates that you will depart Estonia when your visit to the country is complete.

If you are self-employed and run your own business:

- a business permit.
- Your company's most recent six-month bank statement.
- Return of income tax (ITR). evidence that you pay taxes.

If you're in school:

- a letter of approval from your university. demonstrating that after visiting Estonia, you'll go back to your hometown to continue your education.
- If you wish to study in Estonia, you must provide evidence that you have been accepted by the University of Estonia.

Those that have retired:

- Keep a copy of your most recent six-month pension statement.

Minors' Visa Requirements in Estonia

When petitioning for their minor kid, parents or legal guardians must provide the following documentation:

- evidence of parental income. (their company license, a bank statement from the previous six months, an employment contract with evidence of a particular monthly income, etc.)
- a trip authorization form signed by both parents (parent travel consent), regardless of whether they are divorced or apart. The paperwork has to be notarized.

Visa Document Guidelines for Estonia

Your documentation must meet the following requirements when applying for an Estonian visa:

All of your submissions must be in original form, or copies must be certified or notarized.

Translations into Estonian or English are necessary for any paperwork submitted to the embassy or consulate.

An apostille stamp is required on all of your public papers, including marriage certificates, birth certificates, company registration paperwork, and academic degrees.

An apostille stamp may be obtained from an embassy, ministry, court, or regional administration.

What Happens If I Apply Without All The Required Documents?

Your visa application may be rejected if you do not provide all of the desired information from the embassy and submit all necessary paperwork.

You may reapply, challenge the decision, or seek a visa to another Schengen nation if your first application for a visa is denied.

Best Time To Visit Estonia

Recommended time to visit:

With four different seasons, Estonia is a year-round vacation spot.

The hottest months are from June through August in the summer, but if you want to escape the crowds, spring (March through May) and fall (September through October) are better times to visit.

A less well-liked time to go:

Estonia is at its coldest from November to February, yet this may be a fantastic time to go there.

When to go skiing:

Many parts of Estonia have snowfall from November through February, when the ski resorts in the nation begin to operate.

Beach season's best time:

With 3,700 kilometers of Baltic coastline, Estonia is home to several gorgeous seaside towns like Parnu. With bright, sunny days, summer from June through August is the finest season to visit the beach.

Optimum period for wildlife:

Although Estonia is not well recognized for its nature, thousands of migrating and permanent birds arrive there between February and April, making it an ideal location for birdwatchers during this period.

The Ideal 3-Day Trip Itinerary To Estonia

Many tourists that visit the capital of Estonia do so as part of a shore excursion from a cruise ship or as a day trip from Helsinki.

As a result, they only have time to spend a short time in the old town and miss the bulk of what this city has to offer. However, if you have the time, arranging an itinerary for 2 or 3 days in Tallinn is highly recommended to do this city justice.

On the surface, it's simple to believe that one day in Tallinn is sufficient. After all, Tallinn's Old Town, which is the major draw for day visitors, is small and easily walkable in a couple of hours.

However, this not only prevents tourists from enjoying the many sights beyond the Old Town Walls, but it also prevents them from seeing a side of Tallinn that is more typical of city life.

Follow this Tallinn itinerary to experience a side of this magnificent city that many people miss out on if you're interested in acquiring a holistic impression of the Estonian capital!

So, if you've been persuaded to stay in Tallinn for more than a day, you're probably thinking how long to stay there.

Even though Tallinn is not a very big city and it is simple to move about, there is a lot to see and do that you could easily spend three days there and feel like you haven't accomplished everything on your list.

Three days will give you enough time to explore the city for a few days, learn more, and, if you'd like, take a day excursion.

If you don't have the time to dedicate to a lengthier Estonia itinerary, taking a day excursion from Tallinn is a fantastic option to explore more of the nation.

Spending two days in Tallinn is definitely a possibility if you want to see a lot of the city but are a little short on time.

Even though you won't have enough time for a day excursion, you will still be able to spend time in the Old Town, discover Kalamaja and Telliskivi, and, if you so want, visit some museums.

Day 1 – Old Town, Kalamaja & Telliskivi

Tallinn Old Town

Even while it's necessary to go outside of Tallinn's tourist district, no trip to this city would be complete without spending some time in the Old Town, and Tallinn's Old Town is an amazing beauty.

It may get quite crowded since this is the most visited location in Tallinn and the great majority of visitors never leave the city's boundaries.

Remember that Tallinn has a sizable cruise ship terminal and that several ferries bring in enthusiastic day trippers every day.

It might seem incredibly crowded in the Old Town because of how tiny it is. Therefore, it is preferable to get an early start if you desire some tranquility.

Spend the first portion of your Tallinn schedule getting lost and exploring the quaint Old Town. View the Town Hall at Raekoja Plats, the city's central plaza.

Wander over to the Alexander Nevsky Cathedral, a stunning Russian Orthodox building from the 19th century, to appreciate its onion-shaped domes.

Going to some of the observation platforms is an excellent idea as well since you'll get (obviously) fantastic views of the red rooftops and hospital fortifications from there.

For example, the Patkuli Viewing Platform, which offers a panoramic view of the whole ancient portion of the city, is one of the greatest sites to see the town walls.

You may choose to go here for a little price if you're interested in seeing some of the towers and strolling along portions of the walls.

If you want to understand more about the history of medieval Tallinn, there are also a ton of museums and historical sites to see in the Old Town that are well worth visiting.

It may be worthwhile to get a Tallinn Card for individuals who do wish to attend a few fee-based sites, including the city walls, different churches, many museums, the Town Hall tower, and much more.

With this card, you may enter a variety of attractions for free and potentially save a significant amount of money if you want to visit many different ticketed attractions.

Kalamaja

Venture a little beyond the city limits from the Old Town and enter the fashionable Kalamaja district.

Kalamaja has been inhabited since the Middle Ages when it was first built as a residence for fishermen and sailors, however it is not nearly as ancient as the ancient Town. Kalamaja is an Estonian word that means "fish house"!

Since it underwent major gentrification recently, Kalamaja has become a popular destination for many young residents. There are many hip boutique stores, flea markets, parks, cafés, and pubs in the neighborhood!

Even though it only takes five to ten minutes to walk from the city walls to the district, it is quite quiet and seems like a whole other universe from the Old Town.

The tranquil alleyways of Kalamaja, famous for their wooden buildings constructed around the turn of the 20th century, may be explored for several hours.

If you want to escape the higher rates you'll probably find in the Old Town, Kalamaja might be a nice spot to have a snack or a dinner. Consider visiting the Kalamaja Bakery if you're looking for a relaxed, neighborhood spot.

Consider going to Rohe Kohvik if you're looking for something a little more trendy. This vegan café has a ton of great alternatives that may satisfy both "flexitarians" and those on plant-based diets.

Creative City Telliskivi

Telliskivi Creative City, the pinnacle of Tallinn's gentrification in recent years, is located between Kalamaja and the Old Town. With many events, a ton of street art, more upscale stores and eateries, and a flea market every Saturday, the old industrial complex is now the center of the trendy, creative life in the capital of Estonia.

Telliskivi is the ideal location to round off your first day in Tallinn since there are a ton of interesting sites to explore, a ton of art to view, and a ton of places to have a drink or something to eat.

If you're searching for a spot to get a drink, think about visiting the Purtse taproom, which sells beverages from the country's easternmost brewery.

Or, if you're searching for something a little more distinctive, the neighboring Junimperium Distillery & Bar distills its own gin and offers a variety of cocktails, as well as the unusual local fruit wines and spritzes available at the Nudist Winery.

There are a ton of eateries to choose from for supper. There are many excellent possibilities in F-Hoone, which is a very well-liked option. Another fantastic alternative is Kivi Paber

Käärid, where all of their cuisine is fully gluten-free.

Day 2 – Tallinn Harbour and Balti Jaama Turg

Museum of Seaplane Harbour

On your second day in Tallinn, there are several attractions to explore north of the Old Town, including the Patarei Prison, the Seaplane Harbour, and Linnahall.

The Seaplane Harbour Museum in Tallinn is a terrific option if you're traveling with children, but it's also a fantastic place to visit for people of all ages!

The museum, built in a former seaplane hangar, has exhibits on Estonia's nautical history; on the harborfront, numerous ships may be viewed! While access to the museum and ships is included in a ticket that costs €15, admission to the ships is just €6. Children's and student tickets are less costly.

Patarei Prison Museum

The Seaplane Harbour is just a short walk away from Patarei Prison. The prison was first built in the 19th century as a fortress, but it gained notoriety when it started to be used as one in the Soviet period in 1920.

It was used as a prison until the beginning of the twenty-first century; since that time, it has remained vacant.

Since then, Patarei and Estonia during the Soviet period may be learned more about by visiting the jail's museum, which has been converted from a prison.

The whole museum can be explored in about an hour since it is so nicely laid out. Keep in mind that it is rather heavy and could not be suitable for younger children.

Since the museum is now only open at certain periods of the year, make sure it is operational before visiting. There are discounts available for children, students, elderly, and other groups; entry is €8, however.

Linnahall

To reach Linnahall Concert Hall, a similarly derelict Soviet-era structure, take a walk from Patarei Prison. It was built for the Moscow 1980 Summer Olympics, during which Tallinn hosted some sailing contests, but it has since been mostly ignored.

Like many other crumbling concrete structures across the world, it has become a favorite site for locals to meet up with friends and relax while enjoying a few drinks and the harbor.

It's crucial to go as soon as possible since, similar to Patarei Prison, there have been several discussions on restoring this wonderful piece of land in the future.

If you want a location to relax and have a drink nearby, think about traveling to Uba Ja Humal. Various Estonian artisan beers are available for purchase at this taproom and bottle shop.

If you wish to take a longer walk, you might also visit the Phjala Brewery taproom, which is a little bit closer to the seaplane port museum.

Balti Jaama Turg

Go away from the coast and toward the Tallinn train station, where Balti Jaama Market is located, if all the exploring has whetted your hunger. Tallinn's freshly renovated market is a fantastic social melting pot with something for everyone.

Residents may be seen eating at their favorite restaurant as well as buying fresh fruit for their weekly shopping. There are several food booths where you may stop for a snack, and you can choose from a variety of cuisines.

BaoJaam is a particularly well-liked substitute where consumers may choose from a range of bao buns. One of the best vegan burgers I've ever tasted was at Veg Machine, and it would satisfy even the most ardent carnivores.

On the top floor of Balti Jamma Turg is a significant flea market similar to those in other major former Soviet cities. This is a good place to window shop, spend some time browsing about antiques and kitsch, or buy something to remember your two days in Tallinn by.

Day 3 – Lahemaa National Park Day Trip or Pirita

If you only have two days in Tallinn, the two days that have previously been covered will provide you a great introduction to the city.

However, it's worthwhile to add Pirita, the Estonian History Museum, and Lahemaa National Park to your itinerary if you're lucky enough to spend three days in Tallinn.

Lahema National Park

If you have three days in Tallinn, go to the Lahemaa National Park. Lahemaa, famous for its spectacular bogs and stunning beaches, is about

40 minutes from the center of Tallinn. If you have a car, you may visit each separately.

The Lahemaa National Park's main draw, the Viru Bog, is accessible through public transit (board bus 155 from Balti Jaam).

The bog walk is a 6-kilometer route, but if you're carrying small children in a stroller or have mobility challenges, the first kilometer has been made wheelchair and other mobility assistance accessible. The walk is pleasant and quite easy.

If you have your own car or would want to go on a guided tour (this full-day tour is a great alternative), there are further possibilities, including the scenic Vosu, which has a lovely beach, and the Jagala waterfall.

Pirita Maarjamäe & Estonian History Museum

If you choose to stay in the city on your last day in Tallinn, you may visit Pirita and the Estonian History Museum.

Both of these attractions are a bit outside of the city center of Tallinn, so you will need to use public transit to get there.

Fortunately, buying tickets is straightforward. The easiest method is to buy QR tickets online and scan them as you board the bus.

Take any Maarjamägi-bound bus to go to the Estonian History Museum in Maarjamäe. The main reason we went there was because of the Soviet Monuments in the grounds behind the museum.

Lenin and Stalin are only two of the famous Soviet leaders and political figures whose statues can be located here.

As a result of their continued destruction, some of the sculptures are missing body parts, while others are just losing their heads.

The museum houses an exhibition on the last 100 years of Estonian history since the creation of an independent Estonian state.

You may also go to Tallinn's Great Guild Hall in the Old Town and other museums with interesting exhibits.

In the summer, use the same bus you used to get there to Pirita Beach if you're spending your last three days in Tallinn. Pirita Beach is a great city beach where you may relax on a sunny day.

If you only have two days in Tallinn, the two days that have previously been covered will provide you a great introduction to the city.

However, it's worthwhile to add Pirita, the Estonian History Museum, and Lahemaa National Park to your itinerary if you're lucky enough to spend three days in Tallinn.

Lahemaa National Park

If you have three days in Tallinn, go to the Lahemaa National Park. Lahemaa, famous for its spectacular bogs and stunning beaches, is about 40 minutes from the center of Tallinn. If you have a car, you may visit each separately.

The Lahemaa National Park's main draw, the Viru Bog, is accessible through public transit (board bus 155 from Balti Jaam).

The bog walk is a 6-kilometer route, but if you're carrying small children in a stroller or have mobility challenges, the first kilometer has been made wheelchair and other mobility assistance accessible. The walk is pleasant and quite easy.

If you have your own car or would want to go on a guided tour (this full-day tour is a great alternative), there are further possibilities, including the scenic Vosu, which has a lovely beach, and the Jagala waterfall.

Pirita Maarjamäe & Estonian History Museum

If you choose to stay in the city on your last day in Tallinn, you may visit Pirita and the Estonian History Museum.

Both of these attractions are a bit outside of the city center of Tallinn, so you will need to use public transit to get there. Fortunately, buying tickets is straightforward. The easiest method is to buy QR tickets online and scan them as you board the bus.

Take any Maarjamägi-bound bus to go to the Estonian History Museum in Maarjamäe. The main reason we went there was because of the Soviet Monuments in the grounds behind the museum.

Lenin and Stalin are only two of the famous Soviet leaders and political figures whose statues can be located here.

As a result of their continued destruction, some of the sculptures are missing body parts, while others are just losing their heads.

The museum houses an exhibition on the last 100 years of Estonian history since the creation of an independent Estonian state. You may also go to Tallinn's Great Guild Hall in the Old Town and other museums with interesting exhibits.

In the summer, use the same bus you used to get there to Pirita Beach if you're spending your last three days in Tallinn. Pirita Beach is a great city beach where you may relax on a sunny day.

Estonia Travel Cost

A 7-day vacation to Tallinn costs, on average, $1,110 for a single traveler, $1,994 for a couple, and $3,737 for a family of four.

While most vacation rentals cost between $120 and $320 per night for the full property, Tallinn hotels vary from $30 to $152 per night with an average of $75.

The average price of a trip from anywhere in the globe to Helsinki Vantaa Airport (HEL) is between $617 and $979 per person for first class and $1,936 to $3,072 for economy.

We advise setting up $32 to $60 per person each day, depending on the activities, for transportation and dining out at nearby restaurants.

The Most Affordable Seasons to Visit Tallinn, EE

The most affordable times to go to HEL and stay in a hotel in Tallinn are often the following dates: January 1 through March 31 April 23 through May 20 (apart from the week of April 30)

between October 1 and December 9 Early November is often the best time to go to Tallinn on a budget.

Cheap flights to Tallinn

How affordable can a trip to Tallinn be? For those prepared to take standby flights, put up with the hassle, and generally keep travel costs to a minimum, a vacation to Tallinn will cost roughly $81 per person per day.

Vacation rentals may be reserved for as little as $20 per night, or around 3% of total rentals are available for between $0 and $100.

These low-cost accommodations must be reserved as soon as possible and may not be in the most attractive locations.

There are more likely to be 1-star hotels available, with rates beginning at around $26. Depending on where you live and if you can drive, even more affordable excursions may be available.

Cost of a flight to Tallinn

Prices for international flights range from an average high of $979 in early August to a low of $617 in early November.

The average cost of a flight is $667. Millions of flights were used to get these rates. Our data for Tallinn comprises 169 airlines and 287 originating airports.

Compared to other places, the neighborhood has a wider pricing range. The average round-trip flight to Tallinn from Stewart International (SWF) in Newburgh/Poughkeepsie, NY, the United States, is $9,859.

This is far more expensive than the average fare from Oulu (OUL) in Oulu, Finland, which is just $86.
Tuesday is generally the cheapest day to fly in, and Tuesday is usually the cheapest day to fly out.

By following our free flight advice and making an early reservation, you can easily save approximately 59% in Tallinn, where the difference between the cheapest and most costly week is almost $362.

Budget for Daily Expenses

Depending on what you want to accomplish during your trip, your daily costs may vary significantly. A normal decent lunch may cost roughly $14 per person, yet a fine dining restaurant with cocktails in Tallinn might easily charge $210 per person or more.

Although self-guided trips to visit the outdoor attractions might be free, private tours can cost $419 per day. Recommendations are provided based on the cost of living and averages we see for this kind of trip since costs vary greatly.

Cultural Do's & Don'ts

I developed a feeling of what may be considered suitable behavior or conduct and what might be regarded disrespectful or even harmful after having spent the previous few months in Estonia.

Perhaps the information in this blog will be useful to people who want to visit Estonia in the near future (remember: Ryanair will soon provide direct flights from Bremen to Tallinn!). Dos and Don'ts to avoid during your vacation include:

When smoking, avoid taking your cigarette box outdoors. If you do this, you'll probably find yourself in a scenario where three males are "asking" you for one, two, or three cigarettes. Say you are "terribly sorry" and pretend you forgot your package inside.

I very recently developed this practice after calculating that I must have distributed about 4 of these bundles throughout the preceding months.

Do consume Kefir together with Vana Tallinn. Do it now. I truly dislike kefir, but it's essential to drink it in a glass with the greatest vodka from Estonia!

Avoid interfering with the Russians. Sadly, after 20 years since Estonia's independence from the USSR, the Russian community there has scarcely assimilated.

The Estonian government's efforts seem futile, but I'd like to believe that many Russians lack the will to adjust to the "new" independent Estonia.

I've had a lot of run-ins with Russians who would stir up commotion in the neighborhood throughout my stay.

Even my other students who reside in the dorm with me seem uninterested in merely saying "hi" to one another. Up to 95% of people in certain places, including Narva in the north-east, speak Russian.

I don't want to diss Russians in general—the ones I've met and know are some of the nicest people on the planet—but the ones I saw in Tartu and Tallinn I'd prefer not to see again.

Pay attention to Estonian Karaoke singers. A brief period of doubt is only for entertainment purposes. Fun because they play songs from the west in Estonian (since western music was prohibited for a very long time under the USSR), and amazement at the performers' ineptitude.

Don't imagine that Germany is chilly. It's freezing in Estonia! I once awoke around 10 or so in the morning to a temperature of -21°C. You essentially have no choice but to remain indoors and sip tea after tea in that type of weather.

I must be very cautious not to walk outdoors with damp hair since my beard quickly became frozen. I could easily snap one or two dreadlocks:). Therefore, Germany, I really like the weather right now.

Come to Estonia right now! This is the time to be there. It's a nation from where one most likely has little preconceived notions or expectations, thus every day brings fresh perspectives! I've never looked back and regretted coming here. You'll experience it, too! Be quick!

Culture and social etiquette in Estonia

Religion

For the majority of Estonians, religion evolved into a tacit form of resistance throughout the Soviet era.

Religious groups have reappeared after independence.

The Estonian Evangelical Lutheran Church is the biggest church.

The major churches created the Council of Estonian Churches (CEC) in 1989 to bring the various churches together and encourage everyone in Estonia to grow spiritually.

The Function of Families

The family continues to be the center of social life.
Although this is a loose generalization, families are often "nuclear" in cities and "extended" in rural regions.

Due to strong family connections, newlyweds often stay with their parents until they can support themselves, and the elderly are typically cared for rather than being placed in nursing institutions.

The structure of Estonian society

Estonian society is hierarchical.
Respect comes with experience, position, and age.
In general, older individuals are respected and appreciated because they are seen to be wiser.

Elders are presented first and often given royal treatment.

Senior leaders are expected to make judgments that are in the best interests of the whole.

Titles are crucial when addressing someone because of seniority.

Prior to being asked to use someone's first name, it is anticipated that you would use their title and last name.

Cultural Customs

The identity of Estonian culture is quite strong.

During the Soviet era, oral traditions in particular were crucial in maintaining traditions, tales, and rituals.

The "Singing Revolution" of 1989–1991 is recognized for the Estonians' ability to sing their way to freedom. Singing is a distinctively Estonian hobby.

Manners

The majority of Estonians are reserved and quiet.
They often talk gently and dislike making a scene for themselves.

Being calm, logical, and avoiding emotional extremes are all respectable traits.
Estonians may first come across as distant. As a relationship develops, this becomes less of an issue.

Estonian etiquette and manners

Meeting and Salutation

It's possible for greetings to come out as stiff and guarded.
When welcoming ladies, males should always go first, and the younger person should always welcome the elder person.

establish sure to stand up when you meet someone, establish eye contact up front, and provide a warm, strong handshake.

The most typical salutation is "there" (a.k.a. "hello").
Titles have a crucial role. "Härra" stands for Mr., "Prova" for Mrs., and "Preili" for Miss. The surname should be used after everything.
Once you've been accepted to, use first names only.

Etiquette for Giving Gifts

At Christmas and other birthdays, gifts are often given and received.
Gifts don't have to be pricey since the value is more in the idea than the actual value.

Bringing a box of chocolates or some flowers is a respectable present if you are welcomed to an Estonian's home.

Odd numbers should be used when giving flowers.

Gifts are often unwrapped right away.

Dining Manners

Show up on time. Being on time is anticipated. If you're going to be late, call.

Verify if anybody is wearing shoes inside the home.

Homes are private; thus, do not anticipate being given a tour.

Dress sartorially.

Try to volunteer to assist the hostess with the meal's preparation or clean up afterward. This is courteous even if it will be declined.

Don't talk about business.

Any courtesy shown should be reciprocated.

Table etiquette

In Estonia, table manners are generally formal. Until you are requested to sit down, keep standing.

Continental table etiquette dictates that the fork should be held in the left hand when eating and the knife in the right.

Once the hostess begins or someone says "head is" ("good appetite"), you may start eating.
Take care not to rest your elbows on the table.
Thank the hostess for the delicious supper.
Try to complete all the tasks at hand.

Tipping

Although it is not required, Estonian culture dictates that excellent restaurant service should be rewarded with a 10% tip.
Other service providers usually take tips if they are given, but they are not required (for example,

by rounding up the cab cost or by offering a little tip to the porter and cleaner).

Estonian Business Etiquette and Culture

Estonian Protocol for Meeting and Greeting

Due to their formal demeanor, Estonians may not come off as particularly warm or even pleasant to those from more casual cultures.

This should not be taken in that way.
The communication style changes significantly as the connection develops.

Speak to everyone in the room and extend your hand.
Recall that it is impolite to welcome someone when they are sitting.

Handshakes ought to be strong and assured.
Hold sustained eye contact as you briskly shake hands.

Wait for a lady to reach out her hand.

Businesspeople should be addressed by their surname and professional title.

Use "Härra" to address a male and "Prova" to address a woman if they do not have a professional title.

Before using first names, wait until you've been invited.

Business Card Protocol

We exchange business cards casually and without ceremony.

Display your business card so the recipient can read it.

Respectfully handle someone's business card.

It's a kind gesture to have the back of your card translated into Estonian.

Style of Communication

Estonians are sincere communicators who follow through on their promises.
They depend on foreign entrepreneurs to honor their commitments.

A commercial connection may suffer irreversible damage if this is not done.
They usually talk courteously.

Particularly when building a commercial partnership at the beginning, Estonians tend to be somewhat reserved and pragmatist.

Estonians don't talk with much emotion.
If you come from a culture where hand gestures are frequent, you may want to tone them down to fit in with customs where you are.

It's customary to speak softly. When doing business with Estonians, you may want to lower your voice if it is loud.

Especially if they are uncomfortable with the topic or need more time to gather their views, Estonians don't always reply to what has been stated.

Estonians are straightforward communicators, yet they regulate their bluntness to respect everyone's sentiments.

They take their time to congratulate others and may become wary of compliments that are given too quickly or without adequate justification.

A large aspect of the communication approach is passive quiet.
People that interrupt an Estonian while they are speaking will not be well received by them since they dislike conversational overlap.

Estonians are proud of their excellent names. Therefore, take care to avoid openly criticizing or embarrassing somebody.

Etiquette for Business Meetings

The most senior Estonian present usually gives a welcome statement to start meetings. The team member with the greatest experience should make a brief speech in response.

Meetings often continue into lunch or dinner, however the topic will usually be more social than professional.

These ostensibly casual events provide your Estonian coworkers a chance to get to know you personally and develop personal bonds.

Consider the time spent at meals as significant as the time spent at the negotiating table since this is a culture where people like to conduct business with friends.

Although Estonians often mix work and pleasure, it's crucial to maintain a proper approach in meetings.

Estonians disapprove of a too casual approach to business, particularly from visitors.

A choice usually requires multiple meetings. Since choices are still often taken at the top of the organization, unless you are meeting with that group, your proposal will need to be approved further up the chain of command.

Older entrepreneurs often only speak Estonian or Russian fluently. As a result, you may want to bring an interpreter to meetings.

Accommodations in Estonia

Kreutzwald Hotel Tallinn

Value Chic: A stylish option with a superb restaurant and spa facilities in the center of historic Tallinn.

Great walks - Stroll through the charming alleyways of Tallinn's old town to gain a sense of this ancient settlement.
Nearby Attractions: The Estonian National Library is a stunning structure that is well worth seeing.
Good for couples since it is romantic
74 rooms from £64

Merchant's House Hotel

City Style - A historic building in a prime downtown position with ultra-modern interiors.

closest Attractions: Town Hall Square Boutique Restaurant is among the closest attractions.

37 rooms from £78

Merchant's House Hotel

The Von Stackelberg Hotel

Spa getaways - The hotel has a posh Zen spa that combines modern practices with Asian ideas.

Local exploration - The location is ideal for walking around the Old Town.

Great walks - Take a stroll around the Old Town of Tallinn, a UNESCO World Heritage Site, with its cobblestone streets.

Nearby attractions include Toompea Castle and Nevsky Cathedral, which are both just a few feet away.

43 rooms from £90

The Von Stackelberg Hotel

Savoy Boutique

Nearby Savoy Boutique Attractions: 300 m from Town Hall Square Restaurant; recommended.
Boutique Traditional
41 rooms from £133

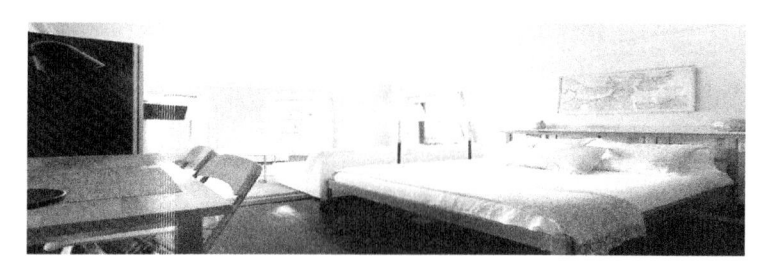

Savoy Boutique

Hotel St Petersburg

Enjoy either Estonian or Russian food at the two on-site eateries, City Style Restaurant.
Located in the center of Tallinn's Old Town, close by attractions
Local markets are great for obtaining local flavor.
27 rooms from £121

Hotel St Petersburg

Schlosele Hotel

City Style - In Tallinn's Old Town, a quaint hotel offers luxuries like car service and sparkling champagne with breakfast.

Local attractions include the ancient Tallinn Old Town, a UNESCO World Heritage Site, and it's cafés, restaurants, pubs, and stores, all of which are within a 10-minute walk.

Great walks: Take a stroll along a portion of Tallinn Town Wall, which resembles a fairytale.
Lively - Trendy and popular.
23 rooms from £129

Telegraaf Hotel

Sailing - The hotel offers boat and yacht excursions in the Tallinn Gulf.
Neary Attractions: Picturesque St. Catberine's Passage will be reached shortly.
Spah and a swimming pool inside
86 rooms from £158

Three Sisters Hotel

With slate flooring, antique wood beams, modern materials, and a modern design, the City Style strikes the ideal balance between the old and the new.

Enjoy a six-course dinner in the kitchen while watching the chef prepare it after a shared bath in the tub as part of a romantic getaway.

Local attractions - Just five minutes away, the historic town square is conveniently located for exploration.
Lively - Trendy and popular.
23 rooms from £147

Three Sisters Hotel

Transportation in Estonia

The free public transportation system, which went into effect in 2013, is the most significant aspect of public transportation in Estonia. As a result of Estonia's free public transportation, its residents benefit.

The scenario has greatly pleased Estonians. Free public transportation across the nation has benefited the government, not hurt it.

Due to the country's free public transit, people began to travel and explore more. The domestic market was therefore opened up, and beneficial economic benefits were produced.

Despite the fact that public transportation is free in Estonia, the country's government has seized a portion of its residents' income tax payments totaling €1000.

First off, only Tallinn, the nation's capital, has free public transit, which was first introduced in test towns.

Additionally, more individuals are traveling to Tallinn to live or work as a result of the city's free public transportation.

The Estonian government's tax income increased by 1 million euros as a result of this rise in population.

Which Estonian public transportation is free?

Buses, trams, and trolleybuses are all forms of free public transportation in Estonia. Even though rail travel is considered public transportation in Estonia, it is not free. Although they are not free in the nation, train tickets are quite affordable.

The state does not presently have any intentions to make the trains free to use. In Estonia, there are many free public transportation options.
Tram Bus
electric trolleybus (buses propelled by electricity poles)

What Advantages Do Free Public Transportation Services Offer in Estonia?

Both Estonians and the Estonian government's economy may benefit from free transportation in that country.

Free public transportation has encouraged people to use their cars less, and numerous bike lanes and dedicated bus lanes have been constructed around the nation to further this goal.

Every year, new residents may join the city since transportation is provided free of charge in Estonia. In this instance, it helps the public treasury save almost one million euros per year.

Every new city resident in Estonia must pay 2 euros for public transportation. In Estonia, people on tight budgets profited significantly from this approach. People were able to start saving money thanks to the free transportation.

In Estonia, free public transportation has boosted mobility inside the city, which has led to increased consumer spending and a resurgence of the economy.

How Much Do Non-Estonian Citizens Pay for Public Transportation?

While it is free for Estonian residents to use the public transportation system, visitors are not entitled to this privilege. For visitors who are younger than 7, public transportation is also free throughout the nation.

Visitors may travel across Estonia via trolleybuses, buses, and trams. From six in the morning to eleven at night, buses travel across the nation. A ticket must be paid in order to use public transportation.

Passengers who are caught without a ticket must face a 40 euro fine. Having a Tallinn Card is the most cost-effective method to use public transportation in the nation.

With this card, you may travel for free to 40 different tourist destinations and utilize all public transit systems. Even some stores and restaurants provide travelers who present this card discounts.

The following are the Tallinn Card fees:
$25 per person for a whole day.
48 hours at 37 euros per person
The cost for 72 hours is 45 euros per person.
The Smart Card is an additional card used for public transit. For the Smart Card, a 2-euro deposit is required.

This deposit is valid for 6 months. The only services offered by Smart Card are public transportation. Smart Card costs include:

3 euros for a whole day.

72 hours for five euros

5 days for 6 euros

1 single ticket, 2 euros

What additional modes of transportation are there in Estonia besides public transit?

Except for public transportation, personal vehicles or taxis are utilized for local transportation in Estonia. Taxi meter rates in Tallinn, the capital of Estonia, start at 5.5 euros. The rate for the cab is 1.1 euros per mile.

Taxi prices across the nation vary. Estonian public transportation Although it is utilized, the majority of those who don't wish to use it commute by bicycle. Cycling is widespread, particularly in the spring and summer. It promotes riding on Estonia's bicycle trails.

Safety and Security

Even yet, there is a little amount of minor criminality. In Tallinn's Old Town, pickpocketing is an issue that occurs when visitors are targeted for their passports and cash.

Be cautious when entering pubs, don't leave your drink alone, take basic safety measures, and stay away from dark parks and side streets after dark. Leave your valuables in a hotel safe if at all feasible.

You should go in person to the Tallinn Central Police Station to report a theft.

Public transportation

Buses, trolleybuses, trams, and inner-city trains in Tallinn all employ a plastic smartcard and electronic ticketing system.

There are several affordable and accessible taxis. Uber, Taxigo, and other transportation-related applications are also commonly utilized.

Make sure that the taxi has a pricing list on the rear window, the driver has a visible driver's license, a visible meter, and that the meter is in operation.

Use registered taxis only; unregistered cabs are unlawful, dangerous, and sometimes far more expensive. Avoid phony cabs at all costs at Tallinn Passenger Port.

Travel by road

In Estonia, there were 52 traffic fatalities in 2019. This is equivalent to 3.9 road fatalities per 100,000 people, which is higher than the 2019 UK average of 2.6 road fatalities per 100,000 people.

Documents and licenses

A UK driver's license is valid for driving in Estonia. If you're traveling by car into Estonia, you must have the original V5C vehicle registration papers.

Foreign use of a British vehicle

If you want to drive your automobile abroad, you may require a UK sticker. UK stickers have taken the place of GB stickers as of September 28, 2021.

Restrictions on driving

Vehicle headlights are required to always be on by law, even when it's daytime.

Every year, from December 1 to March 1, winter tires must be installed; however, if there are severe weather conditions outside of these dates (expected in most years), the dates will modify as necessary. If you want to drive in Estonia between October and April, be sure to check the local conditions.

Don't drive after drinking. Zero is the set legal limit. Those who are discovered to be above the limit risk being fined and/or imprisoned.

In the winter

In the winter (October to March), be ready for severely cold and perhaps dangerous weather. Snow is expected to cover the ground, and it might be as cold as -25°C.

Best Restaurants In Estonia

The caliber and diversity of the eateries in Tallinn, Estonia, cannot not but wow you. There is something for everyone, from modern cuisine to traditional Estonian meals.

If you anticipated hefty Estonian cuisine, you'll be pleasantly surprised by the delectable meals and healthful recipes you'll find here. Continue reading for our suggestions for the top dining establishments in Tallinn.

Estonian Cuisine

Potatoes, wild mushrooms, handmade bread, and Estonian cheese are often seen in traditional Estonian meals. There is no one dish that represents Estonia. However, sprats on black bread and räim, or filets of Baltic herring, are also well-liked dishes.

A multiplier, a kind of pearl barley and potato porridge that is sometimes eaten with bacon, is another classic Estonian dish. It should not be confused with mulgikapsad, a pork dish made in Estonia with sauerkraut and barley.

One of the best sweets in Estonia is apple cake, which is served with curd cheese and berries on top. There are many great craft beers to taste and microbreweries are commonplace around the nation.

Since the 1400s, Estonian vodka has been made, and it is today recognized as a Protected Geographical Indication (PGI). This indicates that all of the raw materials and water used in its production are from Estonia.

Another well-known beverage in Estonia is the Vana Tallinn liqueur. This 1960-released spicy liqueur tastes well on the rocks or in cocktails and is made with rum, herbs, spices, oranges, and lemons.

Best Dining in Tallinn

Tallinn is the ideal location if you want to sample delicious cuisine. Modern Estonian food is offered at several excellent places at reasonable pricing.

In this little city, there are also a lot of quaint coffee shops and taverns with live music. Here is our list of some of Tallinn's top eateries that we have personally experienced.

Restoran LEE

LEE, previously known as Lieb Restaurant, is one of Tallinn's greatest restaurants and is located in the Old Town. It's a nice spot to eat in the summer since it has a big courtyard area.

The old Estonian fires, around which people would gather to prepare meals, are where the name LEE comes from. A wonderful assortment of modern Estonian appetizers sets the tone for the meal.

Main meals like Pähkla fish with new potatoes, fermented potato sauce, green beans, fennel, and lovage oil are served after these. One of the restaurant's specialties is the black bread.

Desserts include a creamy broad bean sorbet with roasted barley broth, redcurrant rhubarb jam, and lemon thyme, among other intriguing options.

The charming Estonian eatery Lore Bistro is run by chefs Janno Lepik and Kristjan Peaske and is located in Tallinn's eccentric Kalamanji neighborhood. In an old shipyard near Noblessner Harbor, Lore serves a variety of food cooked in a wood-fired oven.

Restoran LEE

Restaurant Noa

Noa is the shining gem of Estonian cuisine, with a magnificent setting with views of Tallinn Bay.

Some claim that Noa would most certainly have at least two stars if Estonia had the Michelin star system. There are three levels total, as well as the Noa Chef's Hall, where guests may enjoy a complete tasting menu.

Restaurant Noa

Kaks Kokka Restaurant

You can't go wrong with Kaks Kokka for a comfortable lunch or supper with kind service. Its name translates to "The Two Chefs," and it is run by Saaremaa-native chefs Martin Meikas and Ranno Paukson.

A few doors down from the well-known Restaurant, which is run by the same company, is an unpretentious eatery in Tallinn. Without a doubt, Kaks Kokka is among the top restaurants in Tallinn.

Everything about the setting is laid-back, from the plush couches to the exposed brick walls. We heartily endorse the spicy cheese mousse from Kolotsi with "black dirt" and roasted and seasoned veggies from South Estonia as an appetizer.

Along with the quail from Järveotsa farm served with organic buckwheat from Karmeli farm, the fish dishes here are also excellent.

Pegasus Restaurant

Pegasus stands out for its warm service and cutting-edge food in a contemporary structure on one of the most gorgeous squares in Old Town. The food there is often regarded as the finest in Tallinn, and it tastes just as delicious as it does. The top floor, which has three levels, offers the greatest views.

Pegasus Restaurant

Eating place F-Hoone

F-Huhne is a well-known dining establishment in Kalamaja. It's the height of cool and is situated in an old factory.

The atmosphere is warm and inviting, with brick walls, colorful floor, and orange lighting in the manner of the 1960s.

You should reserve on weekends to avoid having to wait a long time to enter. Halibut filet with pak choi, black olive crumbs, and creamy white bean and celery sauce are just a few of the mouth watering options available.

The locally made coffee is very tasty; if you want something stronger, try the sea buckthorn glögg.

Restaurant Tuljak

Tuljak Restoran, a sibling establishment of Noa, offers expansive views of Tallinn Bay. It is especially well-liked in the summer due to a large patio and outdoor fire pits.

The restaurant, which was initially built in the 1960s, has been completely redone, with modern decor that complements the modernist approach to Estonian cuisine.

A superb range of light nibbles, such as Atlantic herring, greenshell mussels, tiger prawns, and more, are included on the munchies plate for two.

European Bistro

This Tallinn bistro, which should not be mistaken with the Frenchie restaurant in Paris, is housed in a vibrant orange building in the trendy Kalamaja neighborhood.

Sit down next to a Jean-Paul Gaultier impersonator inside. While enjoying French cuisine like Croque Monsieur or Tartiflette, take in the eccentric décor.

European Bistro

Restaurant & Bar Horisont

The opulent Swissôtel Tallinn's Horisont Restaurant & Bar is situated on the 30th floor and offers stunning views of both the Old Town and the sea.

A roomy private dining area, a chic lounge bar, and a restaurant are all present. In the restaurant, the focus is on exquisite cuisine and seasonal, fresh ingredients, while in the bar, Estonian gin is used to mix up distinctive drinks.

Nightlife And Clubs in Estonia

After dark, when all the top nightclubs open their doors and welcome visitors to amazing events, Tallinn really comes to life.

Everyone may find the rhythm they're searching for in Tallinn since there are many clubs to select from, each with its own distinctive atmosphere. These are the top eight clubs in the capital of Estonia.

Tapper, a rock club

The most well-liked location in Tallinn for hard rock enthusiasts that hanker for outstanding live performances is Rockclub Tapper. The top bands from Latvia and Finland join the musicians from Estonia in appearing at Tapper. Only when there is a show booked does this club open.

Amigo Cafe

At Cafe Amigo, which is situated under the Hotel Viru and often draws large audiences, you may let loose to the most popular sounds on other days of the week while dancing to the greatest live artists from Thursday through Saturday. The motto of Cafe Amigo is "Partying is sacred," which ensures that each guest may concentrate on a great party, delectable drinks, and chic dancing movements.

Amigo Cafe

Kelm Kultuuriklubi

If you want a hardcore party, go no further than Tallinn's Kultuuriklubi Kelm, which is a student favorite. However, Kelm offers a lot more activities than simply drinking and dancing.

Visit Kelm and be amazed by how great it is; every night, something new occurs there, such as quizzes, karaoke parties, and poetry readings. Additionally, they provide some of Tallinn's greatest beers, so visit the pub and sample as many as you can.

After dark, when all the top nightclubs open their doors and welcome visitors to amazing events, Tallinn really comes to life.

Everyone may find the rhythm they're searching for in Tallinn since there are many clubs to select from, each with its own distinctive atmosphere.

These are the top eight clubs in the capital of Estonia.

Privé

Urban music lovers should go to Privé Club in Tallinn since the proprietors take great care to choose the greatest DJs who play the hottest and catchiest tunes. Additionally, the club's staff is quite welcoming, and it is situated in a handy location just adjacent to Freedom Square.

Privé

Vabank

The classiest club in Tallinn is Vabank, thus you should dress up and be above 21 to enter. At Vabank, the elite of Tallinn's entertainment industry celebrate, giving the area a Hollywood vibe. Three distinct dance floors are playing disco, R&B, and pop music, among other genres.

Vabank

Studio Club

One of the top places to go in Tallinn for a fun party with popular rhythms and alternative electro music is Club Studio. Make sure to arrive early since the club is always packed; otherwise, you can spend the most of your night outdoors waiting in line.

Signaling

Sinilind is a highly reliable club that welcomes its guests to party hard to the greatest DJs in Tallinn. It is situated in the center of Tallinn, just across St. Catherine's Passage. At Sinilind, there are also sporadic activities planned, such as comedy nights.

Venus Club

Given that entry to Venus Club requires that you be at least 21 years old, it is most likely the club that older crowds frequent. During the summer, it is open seven days a week, so if you want to party on a Monday or a Tuesday, Venus Club will provide you a dance floor. Due to the professionalism of the DJs and the rest of the crew, you will always feel at ease and well-cared-for.

Venus Club

Conclusion

Estonia is a fascinating country with a rich cultural heritage, stunning natural beauty, and a thriving arts and culture scene. Whether you're interested in exploring its medieval cities, hiking through its national parks, or experiencing its unique blend of East and West, Estonia has something to offer for everyone.

With its well-preserved medieval Old Town, vibrant nightlife, and delicious local cuisine, the capital city of Tallinn is a popular destination for tourists from around the world.

But Estonia is much more than just its capital city - the country's coastline is dotted with picturesque fishing villages, sandy beaches, and rugged cliffs, making it a great destination for water sports and outdoor activities.

Its national parks, including Lahemaa National Park and Soomaa National Park, are home to a diverse array of wildlife and offer visitors the chance to explore some of Estonia's most beautiful natural landscapes.

Estonia's location at the intersection of Europe and Russia has given it a unique identity and a rich cultural heritage.

Its language, which belongs to the Finno-Ugric language family, is closely related to Finnish and Hungarian and is distinct from the Indo-European languages spoken by its neighboring countries.

This has resulted in a fascinating blend of East and West that is reflected in the country's art, music, and cuisine.

In recent years, Estonia has become a leader in the fields of technology and digital innovation, leveraging its location at the intersection of East and West to become a hub for e-government, cybersecurity, and other areas of digital technology.

This has made Estonia an increasingly popular destination for tech entrepreneurs and investors, as well as for tourists interested in exploring the cutting edge of digital innovation.

Overall, Estonia is a small country with a big impact on the world stage. Whether you're interested in exploring its medieval history, its natural beauty, or its cutting-edge tech industry, Estonia is a destination that should not be missed.

With its friendly locals, rich cultural heritage, and stunning landscapes, Estonia is a truly unique and unforgettable travel destination.

Printed in Great Britain
by Amazon